This book belongs to:

____

Chinese language

The Chinese language differs significantly from Romance languages such as French and Spanish, which are phonetic languages with a set alphabet. Instead, Chinese is made up of thousands of individual characters, each of which has at least one, if not many, meanings.

This is the most significant distinction between Chinese characters and letters used in Western languages.

Chinese Characters

There is more than 85,568 Chinese characters in the world. Is it a big shock? Don't give up immediately. According to the official research of China Education Committee, there are only 3500 commonly used modern Chinese characters, which cover about 99.48% words and characters that you could read in daily life. And you can read around 97.97% of modern everyday Chinese if you know about 2500 characters out of the 3500 characters.

Learning the characters is not a particularly hard part of learning Chinese. But first you need to know what is strokes, radicals and Pinyin.

strokes

Many Chinese learners may believe that Chinese characters are just a jumble of lines and squares that make no sense.

Chinese character is constructed from a number of strokes.

Strokes are the classified set of line patterns that may be arranged and combined to form Chinese characters

Radicals

A character consists of one or more components, called radicals, so a radical is part of a character.

Characters consist of radicals, while radicals consist of strokes. A stroke is the smallest component of a character.

Pinyin

Pinyin is the most commonly used phonetic system for writing Mandarin using the Latin alphabet.

Pinyin is simply the product of transliterating Chinese into romanized spelling.

500 Commonly Used Modern Chinese Characters

It is important to write Chinese characters properly from the beginning.
You probably think learning how to write in Chinese is impossible.
But you're about to learn that it's not impossible.
To make your study more convenient, we provide you the first 500
commonly used Chinese characters list as following.

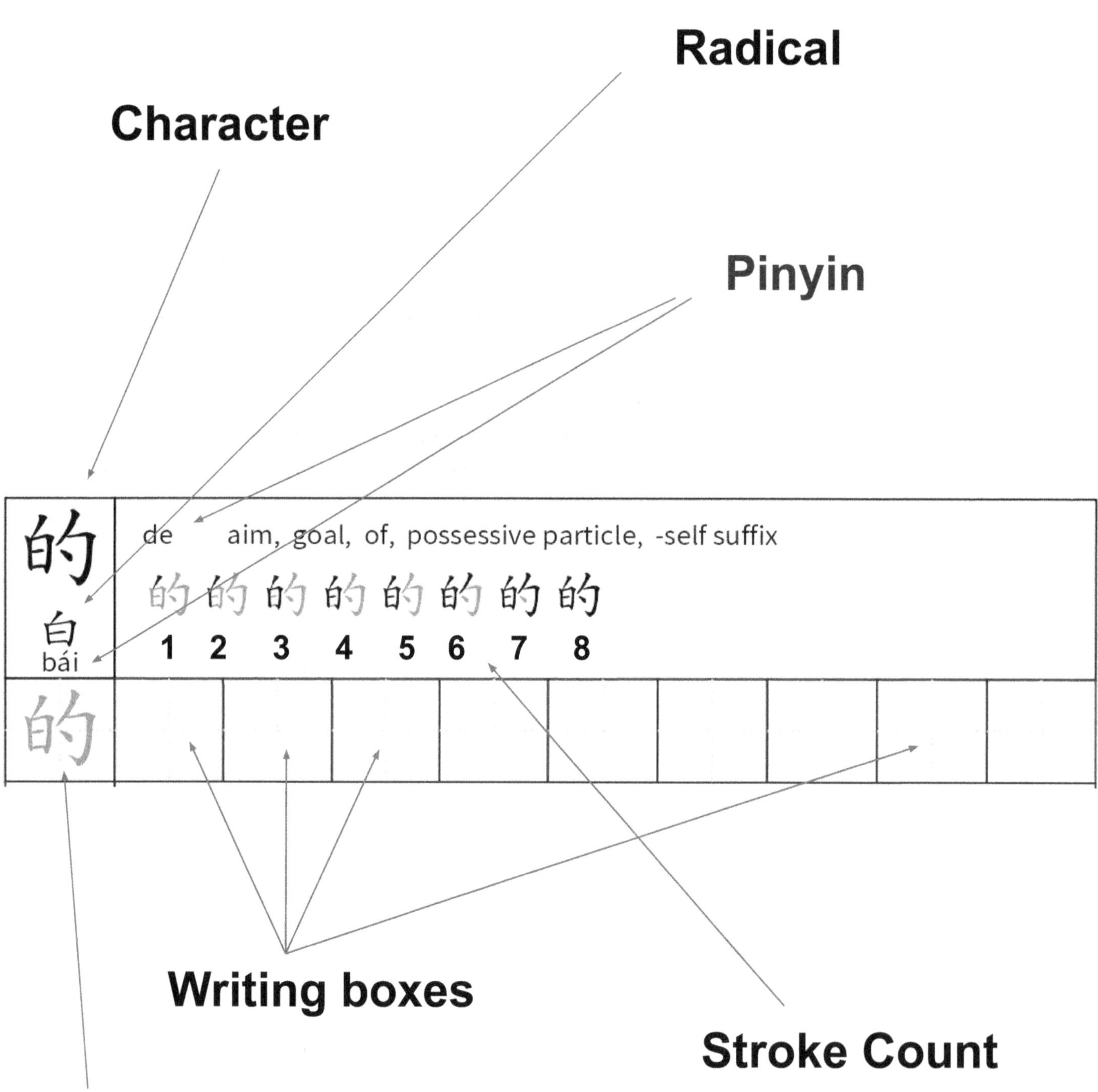

Character
Radical
Pinyin
de   aim, goal, of, possessive particle, -self suffix
bái
1 2 3 4 5 6 7 8
Writing boxes
Stroke Count
Tracing box

的 白 bái	de aim, goal, of, possessive particle, -self suffix 的 的 的 的 的 的 的 的
的	

一 一 yī	yī one, a, an, alone 一
一	

是 日 rì	shì to be, indeed, right, yes, okay 是 是 是 是 是 是 是 是 是
是	

不 一 yī	bù no, not, un-, negative prefix 不 不 不 不
不	

了 亅 jué	le clear, to finish, particle of completed action 了 了
了	

人 人 rén	rén man, person, people 人 人							
人								
我 戈 gē	wǒ I, me, my, our, us 我 我 我 我 我 我 我							
我								
在 土 tǔ	zài at, in, on, to exist, used to indicate the present progressive tense 在 在 在 在 在 在							
在								
有 月 yuè	yǒu to have, to own, to possess, to exist 有 有 有 有 有 有							
有								
他 亻 rén	tā other, another, he, she, it 他 他 他 他 他							
他								

| 这 | zhè   this, these, such, here |
| 辶 chuò | 这 这 这 这 这 这 这 |

| 这 | | | | | | | |

| 中 | zhōng   central, center, middle, amidst, to hit (target), to attain, China |
| 丨 shù | 中 中 中 中 |

| 中 | | | | | | | |

| 大 | dà   big, great, vast, high, deep |
| 大 dà | 大 大 大 |

| 大 | | | | | | | |

| 来 | lái   to arrive, to come, to return, in the future, later on |
| 木 mù | 来 来 来 来 来 来 来 |

| 来 | | | | | | | |

| 上 | shàng   above, on top, superior, to go up, to attend, previous |
| 一 yī | 上 上 上 |

| 上 | | | | | | | |

国 口 wéi	guó　　country, nation, state, national 国 国 国 国 国 国 国 国
国	
个 丨 shù	gè　　this, that, single, measure word for individuals 个 个 个
个	
到 刂 dāo	dào　　to go to, to arrive 到 到 到 到 到 到 到 到
到	
说 讠 yán	shuō　　to speak, to say, to scold, to upbraid 说 说 说 说 说 说 说 说 说
说	
们 亻 rén	men　　plural marker for pronouns and some nouns 们 们 们 们 们
们	

为 、 diǎn	wèi to do, to act, to handle, to govern, to be 为 为 为 为
为	
子 子 zǐ	zi son, child, seed, egg, fruit, small thing 子 子 子
子	
和 口 kǒu	hé harmony, peace, calm, peaceful 和 和 和 和 和 和 和 和
和	
你 亻 rén	nǐ you, second person pronoun 你 你 你 你 你 你 你
你	
地 土 tǔ	de earth, ground, soil, land, region 地 地 地 地 地 地
地	

出	chū to go out, to send out, stand, produce
凵 qiǎn	出 出 出 出 出
出	
道	dào method, way, path, road
辶 chuò	道 道 道 道 道 道 道 道 道 道
道	
也	yě also, too
乚 gōu	也 也 也
也	
时	shí time, season, period, era, age
日 rì	时 时 时 时 时 时 时
时	
年	nián year, anniversary, a person's age
干 gàn	年 年 年 年 年 年
年	

得 彳 chì	dé to obtain, to get, to acquire, suitable, proper, ready
	得 得 得 得 得 得 得 得 得 得 得

就 尢 yóu	jiù just, simply, to go to, to approach, near
	就 就 就 就 就 就 就 就 就 就 就 就

那 阝 yì	nà that, that one, those
	那 那 那 那 那 那

要 覀 xī	yào essential, necessary, to ask for, to coerce, to demand
	要 要 要 要 要 要 要 要 要

下 一 yī	xià below, underneath, inferior, to bring down, next
	下 下 下

| 以 | yǐ — according to, so as to, because of, then |
| 以以以以 |

| 生 | shēng — life, lifetime, birth, growth |
| 生生生生生 |

| 会 | huì — to assemble, to meet, meeting, association, group |
| 会会会会会会 |

| 自 | zì — self, private, personal, from |
| 自自自自自自 |

| 着 | zhe — to make a move, to take action |
| 着着着着着着着着着着 |

去 厶 sī	qù to go away, to leave, to depart 去 去 去 去 去
去	
之 丿 piě	zhī marks preceding phrase as modifier of following phrase, it, him her 之 之 之
之	
过 辶 chuò	guò pass, to go across, to pass through 过 过 过 过 过 过
过	
家 宀 gài	jiā house, home, residence, family 家 家 家 家 家 家 家 家 家 家
家	
学 子 zi	xué learning, knowledge, science, to study, to go to school, -ology 学 学 学 学 学 学 学 学
学	

对 寸 cùn	duì correct, right, facing, opposed 对 对 对 对 对
对								
可 口 kǒu	kě may, can, -able, possibly 可 可 可 可 可
可								
她 女 nǚ	tā she, her 她 她 她 她 她 她
她								
里 里 lǐ	lǐ unit of distance equal to 0.5km, village, lane 里 里 里 里 里 里 里
里								
后 口 kǒu	hòu after, behind, rear, descendants 后 后 后 后 后 后
后								

小 小 xiǎo	xiǎo small, tiny, insignificant 小 小 小
么 丿 piě	me interrogative particle 么 么 么
心 心 xīn	xīn heart, mind, soul 心 心 心 心
多 夕 xī	duō much, many, multi-, more than, over 多 多 多 多 多 多
天 大 dà	tiān sky, heaven, god, celestial 天 天 天 天

而 而 **ér**	**ér** and, and then, and yet, but 而 而 而 而 而 而
而	
能	**néng** can, may, capable, full of energy 能 能 能 能 能 能 能 能 能 能
能	
好 女 **nǚ**	**hǎo** good, excellent, fine, proper, suitable, well 好 好 好 好 好 好
好	
都 阝 **yì**	**dōu** all, each, entirely, whole, metropolis, capital 都 都 都 都 都 都 都 都 都 都
都	
然 灬 **huǒ**	**rán** certainly, naturally, suddenly 然 然 然 然 然 然 然 然 然 然 然 然
然	

| 没
氵
shuǐ | **méi**   not, none, gone, to bury, to sink, to drown
没 没 没 没 没 没 没 |
| 没 | |

| 日
日
rì | **rì**   sun, day, daytime
日 日 日 日 |
| 日 | |

| 于
二
èr | **yú**   at, in, on, to, from, alas!
于 于 于 |
| 于 | |

| 起
走
zǒu | **qǐ**   to begin, to initiate, to rise, to stand up
起 起 起 起 起 起 起 起 起 起 |
| 起 | |

| 还
辶
chuò | **hái**   also, besides, still, yet, to return
还 还 还 还 还 还 还 |
| 还 | |

发 又 yòu	fā　　to issue, to dispatch, to send out, hair
发	发 发 发 发 发
成 戈 gē	chéng　　to accomplish, to become, to complete, to finish, to succeed
成	成 成 成 成 成 成
事 亅 jué	shì　　affair, matter, business, to serve, accident, incident
事	事 事 事 事 事 事 事 事
只 口 kǒu	zhī　　only, merely, just
只	只 只 只 只 只
作 亻 rén	zuò　　to make, to write, to compose, to act, to perform
作	作 作 作 作 作 作 作
作	

| 当 | **dāng**   appropriate, timely, to act, to serve, the sound of bells |
| 当 | 当 当 当 当 当 当 |

| 想
心
xīn | **xiǎng**   to believe, to wish for, to consider, to plan, to think |
| 想 | 想 想 想 想 想 想 想 想 想 想 想 想 |

| 看
目
mù | **kàn**   to look, to see, to examine, to scrutinize |
| 看 | 看 看 看 看 看 看 看 看 看 |

| 文
文
wén | **wén**   culture, literature, writing |
| 文 | 文 文 文 文 |

| 无
无
wú | **wú**   no, not, lacking, -less |
| 无 | 无 无 无 无 |

开 艹 gǒng	kāi to open, to start, to initiate, to begin 开 开 开 开
开	
手 手 shǒu	shǒu hand 手 手 手 手
手	
十 十 shí	shí ten, tenth, complete, perfect 十 十
十	
用 用 yòng	yòng to use, to employ, to apply, use 用 用 用 用 用
用	
主 、 diǎn	zhǔ to own, to host, master, host, lord 主 主 主 主 主
主	

行 行 xíng	xíng to go, to walk, to move, professional 行 行 行 行 行 行							
行								
方 方 fāng	fāng square, rectangle, side, region, flag 方 方 方 方							
方								
又 又 yòu	yòu and, also, again, in addition 又 又							
又								
如 女 nǚ	rú as, as if, like, such as, supposing 如 如 如 如 如 如							
如								
前 刂 dāo	qián in front, forward, former, preceding 前 前 前 前 前 前 前 前 前							
前								

所 户 hù	suǒ place, location, 所 所 所 所 所 所 所 所
所	
本 木 mù	běn root, origin, source, basis 本 本 本 本 本
本	
见 见 jiàn	jiàn to see, to observe, to meet, to appear 见 见 见 见
见	
经 纟 sī	jīng the classics, to experience, to undergo 经 经 经 经 经 经 经 经
经	
头 大 dà	tóu head, chief, boss, first, top 头 头 头 头 头
头	

面 面 miàn	miàn face, surface, side, plane, dimension 面 面 面 面 面 面 面 面 面
面	
公 八 bā	gōng fair, equitable, public, duke 公 公 公 公
公	
同 口 kǒu	tóng same, similar, together with, alike 同 同 同 同 同 同
同	
三 一 yī	sān three 三 三 三
三	
已 己 jǐ	yǐ already, finished, to stop, then, afterwards 已 已 已
已	

老 老 lǎo	lǎo old, aged, experienced 老 老 老 老 老 老
老	
从 人 rén	cóng from, by, since, whence, through 从 从 从 从
从	
动 力 lì	dòng to move, to happen, movement, action 动 动 动 动 动 动
动	
两 一 yī	liǎng two, both, pair, couple, ounce 两 两 两 两 两 两 两
两	
长 长 zhǎng	zhǎng long, lasting, to excel in 长 长 长 长
长	

知 矢 shǐ	zhī to know, to perceive, to comprehend 知 知 知 知 知 知 知 知							
知								
民 民 mín	mín citizens, subjects, a nation's people 民 民 民 民 民							
民								
样 木 mù	yàng form, pattern, shape, style 样 样 样 样 样 样 样 样 样 样							
样								
现 王 wáng	xiàn to appear, to manifest, current, now 现 现 现 现 现 现 现 现							
现								
分 刀 dāo	fēn to divide, to allocate, fraction, small unit of time or other quantity 分 分 分 分							
分								

将 扌 qiáng	jiāng the future, what will be, ready, prepared, a general 将 将 将 将 将 将 将 将 将
将	
外 夕 xī	wài out, outside, external, foreign, in addition 外 外 外 外 外
外	
但 亻 rén	dàn only, but, however, yet, still 但 但 但 但 但 但 但
但	
身 身 shēn	shēn body, torso, person, pregnancy 身 身 身 身 身 身 身
身	
些 二 èr	xiē little, few, rather, somewhat 些 些 些 些 些 些 些 些
些	

与 一 yī	yǔ and, with, to, for, to give, to grant 与 与 与
与	
高 高 gāo	gāo tall, lofty, high, elevated 高 高 高 高 高 高 高 高 高 高
高	
意 心 xīn	yì thought, idea, opinion, desire, wish, meaning, intention 意 意 意 意 意 意 意 意 意 意 意 意
意	
进 辶 chuò	jìn to advance, to make progress, to come in, to enter 进 进 进 进 进 进 进
进	
把 扌 shǒu	bǎ to grasp, to hold, to guard, to take, handle 把 把 把 把 把 把 把
把	

法 氵 shuǐ	fǎ　　law, rule, statute, method, way, French 法 法 法 法 法 法 法 法							
法								
此 止 zhǐ	cǐ　　this, these, in this case, then 此 此 此 此 此 此							
此								
实 宀 gài	shí　　real, true, honest, sincere 实 实 实 实 实 实 实 实							
实								
回 口 wéi	huí　　to return, to turn around, a time 回 回 回 回 回 回							
回								
二 二 èr	èr　　two, twice 二 二							
二								

理 王 wáng	lǐ　　science, reason, logic, to manage 理 理 理 理 理 理 理 理 理 理
理	

美 羊 yáng	měi　　beautiful, pretty, pleasing 美 美 美 美 美 美 美 美 美
美	

点 灬 huǒ	diǎn　　dot, point, speck 点 点 点 点 点 点 点 点 点
点	

月 月 yuè	yuè　　moon, month 月 月 月 月
月	

明 日 rì	míng　　bright, clear, to explain, to understand, to shed light 明 明 明 明 明 明 明 明
明	

其 八 bā	qí his, her, its, their, that 其 其 其 其 其 其 其 其
其	
种 禾 hé	zhǒng race, kind, breed, seed, to plant 种 种 种 种 种 种 种 种 种
种	
声 士 shì	shēng sound, noise, voice, tone, music 声 声 声 声 声 声 声
声	
全 入 rù	quán whole, entire, complete, to preserve 全 全 全 全 全 全
全	
工 工 gōng	gōng labor, work, laborer, worker 工 工 工
工	

己 jǐ	jǐ self, oneself, personal, private, 6th heavenly stem 己 己 己
话 yán	huà talk, speech, language, dialect 话 话 话 话 话 话 话 话
儿 ér	ér son, child 儿 儿
者 lǎo	zhě that which, they who, those who 者 者 者 者 者 者 者 者
向 kǒu	xiàng towards, direction, trend 向 向 向 向 向 向

情 忄 xīn	**qíng** emotion, feeling, sentiment
情	情 情 情 情 情 情 情 情 情 情
部 阝 yì	**bù** department, ministry, division, unit, part, section
部	部 部 部 部 部 部 部 部 部 部
正 止 zhǐ	**zhèng** straight, right, proper, correct, just, true
正	正 正 正 正 正
名 口 kǒu	**míng** name, position, rank, title
名	名 名 名 名 名 名
定 宀 gài	**dìng** to decide, to fix, to settle, to order, definite, fixed, sure
定	定 定 定 定 定 定 定 定

女 女 nǚ	nǚ　　woman, girl, female 女 女 女							
女								
问 门 mén	wèn　　to ask about, to inquire after 问 问 问 问 问 问							
问								
力 力 lì	lì　　strength, power, capability, influence 力 力							
力								
机 木 mù	jī　　desk, machine, moment, opportunity 机 机 机 机 机 机							
机								
给 纟 sī	gěi　　to give, to lend, for, by 给 给 给 给 给 给 给 给 给							
给								

等

děng   rank, grade, same, equal, to wait

等 等 等 等 等 等 等 等 等 等 等 等

几

jǐ   small table, how many, a few, some

几 几

很

hěn   very, quite, much

很 很 很 很 很 很 很 很 很

业

yè   business, profession, to study, to work

业 业 业 业 业

最

zuì   most, extremely, exceedingly, superlative

最 最 最 最 最 最 最 最 最 最 最

| 间
门
mén | jiān   between, among, midpoint, space, place, locality
间 间 间 间 间 间 间 |
| 间 | |

| 新
斤
jīn | xīn   new, recent, fresh, modern
新 新 新 新 新 新 新 新 新 新 新 新 |
| 新 | |

| 什
亻
rén | shén   what? mixed, miscellaneous
什 什 什 什 |
| 什 | |

| 打
扌
shǒu | dǎ   to attack, to beat, to hit, to strike
打 打 打 打 打 |
| 打 | |

| 便
亻
rén | biàn   easy, convenient, expedient
便 便 便 便 便 便 便 便 便 |
| 便 | |

位 亻 rén	wèi seat, throne, rank, status, position, location
	位位位位位位位

位								

因 口 wéi	yīn cause, reason, by, because
	因因因因因因

因								

重 里 lǐ	zhòng heavy, weighty, to double, to repeat
	重重重重重重重重重

重								

被 衤 yī	bèi bedding, a passive particle meaning
	被被被被被被被被被

被								

走 走 zǒu	zǒu to walk, to run, to flee
	走走走走走走走

走								

| 电
日 yuē | diàn   electricity, electric, lightning
电 电 电 电 电 |
| 电 | |

| 四
口 wéi | sì   four
四 四 四 四 四 |
| 四 | |

| 第
竹 zhú | dì   sequence, number, grade, degree, particle prefacing an ordinal
第 第 第 第 第 第 第 第 第 第 第 |
| 第 | |

| 门
门 mén | mén   gate, door, entrance, opening
门 门 门 |
| 门 | |

| 相
目 mù | xiāng   mutual, reciprocal, equal, each other
相 相 相 相 相 相 相 相 相 |
| 相 | |

次 欠 qiàn	cì order, sequence, second, next, one after the other 次 次 次 次 次 次
次	
东 一 yī	dōng east, eastern, eastward 东 东 东 东 东
东	
政 攵 pū	zhèng government, politics 政 政 政 政 政 政 政 政 政
政	
海 氵shuǐ	hǎi sea, ocean, maritime 海 海 海 海 海 海 海 海 海 海
海	
口 口 kǒu	kǒu mouth, entrance, gate, opening 口 口 口
口	

使 亻 rén	shǐ cause, mission, orders, envoy, messenger, ambassador 使 使 使 使 使 使 使 使							
使								
教 攵 pū	jiào school, education 教 教 教 教 教 教 教 教 教 教 教							
教								
西 西 xī	xī west, western, westward 西 西 西 西 西 西							
西								
再 冂 jiōng	zài again, twice, re- 再 再 再 再 再 再							
再								
平 广 guǎng	píng flat, level, even, peaceful 平 平 平 平 平							
平								

真 目 mù	zhēn real, actual, true, genuine 真 真 真 真 真 真 真 真 真 真
听 口 kǒu	tīng to hear, to listen, to understand, to obey 听 听 听 听 听 听 听
世 一 yī	shì generation, era, age, world 世 世 世 世 世
气 气 qì	qì air, gas, steam, vapor, anger 气 气 气 气
信 亻 rén	xìn to trust, to believe, letter, sign 信 信 信 信 信 信 信 信 信

北 匕 bǐ	běi north, northern, northward 北 北 北 北 北							
北								
少 小 xiǎo	shǎo few, little, less, inadequate 少 少 少 少							
少								
关 ha	guān frontier pass, to close, to shut, relation 关 关 关 关 关 关							
关								
并 干 gàn	bìng to combine, to annex, also, what's more 并 并 并 并 并 并							
并								
内 入 rù	nèi inside 内 内 内 内							
内								

| 加 | jiā   to add to, to increase, to augment |
| 力 lì | 加 加 加 加 加 |

| 化 | huà   to change, to convert, to reform, -ize |
| 匕 bǐ | 化 化 化 化 |

| 由 | yóu   cause, reason, from |
| 田 tián | 由 由 由 由 由 |

| 却 | què   still, but, decline, retreat |
| 卩 jié | 却 却 却 却 却 却 却 |

| 代 | dài   era, generation, to substitute for, to replace |
| 亻 rén | 代 代 代 代 代 |

军 车 chē	jūn army, military, soldiers, troops 军 军 军 军 军 军							
军								

产 亠 tóu	chǎn to give birth, to bring forth, to produce 产 产 产 产 产 产							
产								

入 入 rù	rù to enter, to come in, to join 入 入							
入								

先 儿 ér	xiān first, former, previous 先 先 先 先 先 先							
先								

山 山 shān	shān mountain, hill, peak 山 山 山							
山								

五 二 èr	wǔ five, surname 五 五 五 五
五	
太 大 dà	tài very, too much, big, extreme 太 太 太 太
太	
水 水 shuǐ	shuǐ water, liquid, lotion, juice 水 水 水 水
水	
万 一 yī	wàn ten thousand, innumerable 万 万 万
万	
市 巾 jīn	shì city, town, market, fair, to trade 市 市 市 市 市
市	

眼 目 mù	yǎn eyelet, hole, opening 眼 眼 眼 眼 眼 眼 眼 眼 眼 眼 眼
体 亻 rén	tǐ body, group, class, form, style, system 体 体 体 体 体 体 体
别 刂 dāo	bié to separate, to distinguish, to classify, to leave, other, do not 别 别 别 别 别 别 别
处 夂 zhǐ	chù to reside at, to live in, place, locale, department 处 处 处 处 处
总 心 xīn	zǒng to gather, to collect, overall, altogether 总 总 总 总 总 总 总 总 总

才	cái ability, talent, gift, just, only
扌 shǒu	才 才 才
才	
场	chǎng field, open space, market, square, stage
土 tǔ	场 场 场 场 场 场
场	
师	shī teacher, professional, master
巾 jīn	师 师 师 师 师 师
师	
书	shū book, letter, document, writing
丨 shù	书 书 书 书
书	
比	bǐ to compare, liken, comparison, than
比 bǐ	比 比 比 比
比	

住 亻 rén	zhù — to reside, to live at, to dwell, to lodge, to stop 住 住 住 住 住 住 住
员 口 kǒu	yuán — employee, member, personnel, staff 员 员 员 员 员 员 员
九 乙 yǐ	jiǔ — nine 九 九
笑 竹 zhú	xiào — to smile, to laugh, to giggle, to snicker 笑 笑 笑 笑 笑 笑 笑 笑 笑 笑
性 忄 xīn	xìng — sex, nature, character, suffix converting a verb to an adjective 性 性 性 性 性 性 性 性

通	**tōng** to pass through, to open, to connect, to communicate, common
辶 chuò	通 通 通 通 通 通 通 通 通 通
通	

目	**mù** eye, to look, to see, division, topic
目 mù	目 目 目 目 目
目	

华	**huá** flowery, illustrious, Chinese
十 shí	华 华 华 华 华 华
华	

报	**bào** to announce, to report, newspaper, payback, revenge
扌 shǒu	报 报 报 报 报 报 报
报	

立	**lì** to stand, to establish, to set up
立 lì	立 立 立 立 立
立	

马 马 mǎ	mǎ　　horse, surname 马　马　马
马							
命 口 kǒu	mìng　　life, destiny, fate, luck, an order, instruction 命　命　命　命　命　命　命　命
命							
张 弓 gōng	zhāng　　to display, to expand, to open, to stretch, a sheet of paper 张　张　张　张　张　张　张
张							
活 氵 shuǐ	huó　　to exist, to live, to survive, living, working 活　活　活　活　活　活　活　活　活
活							
难 又 yòu	nán　　hard, difficult, arduous, unable 难　难　难　难　难　难　难　难　难
难							

神 礻 shì	shén god, spirit, divine, mysterious, supernatural 神 神 神 神 神 神 神 神 神
神	
数 攵 pū	shù count, number, several 数 数 数 数 数 数 数 数 数 数 数 数 数
数	
件 亻 rén	jiàn item, matter, component, part, measure word for events 件 件 件 件 件 件
件	
安 宀 gài	ān peaceful, tranquil, quiet 安 安 安 安 安 安
安	
表 衣 yī	biǎo to show, to express, to display, outside, appearance, a watch 表 表 表 表 表 表 表 表
表	

原 厂 chǎng	yuán source, origin, beginning 原 原 原 原 原 原 原 原 原 原
原	
车 车 chē	chē cart, vehicle, to move in a cart 车 车 车 车
车	
白 白 bái	bái white, clear, pure, unblemished, bright 白 白 白 白 白
白	
应 广 guǎng	yīng should, must, to respond, to handle, to deal with, to cope 应 应 应 应 应 应 应
应	
路 足 zú	lù road, path, street, journey 路 路 路 路 路 路 路 路 路 路 路 路 路
路	

期 月 yuè	**qī** a period of time, date, time, phase 期 期 期 期 期 期 期 期 期 期 期 期
期	
叫 口 kǒu	**jiào** cry, shout, to call, to greet, to hail 叫 叫 叫 叫 叫
叫	
死 歹 dǎi	**sǐ** dead, death, impassable, inflexible 死 死 死 死 死 死
死	
常 巾 jīn	**cháng** common, general, normal, always, frequently, regularly 常 常 常 常 常 常 常 常 常 常 常
常	
提 扌 shǒu	**tí** to hold in the hand, to lift, to raise 提 提 提 提 提 提 提 提 提 提 提
提	

感 心 xīn 感	gǎn to affect, to move, to touch, to perceive, to sense 感 感 感 感 感 感 感 感 感 感 感
金 金 jīn 金	jīn gold, metal, money 金 金 金 金 金 金 金 金
何 亻 rén 何	hé what, why, where, which, how 何 何 何 何 何 何 何
更 日 yuē 更	gèng more, further, to shift, to alternate, to modify 更 更 更 更 更 更 更
反 又 yòu 反	fǎn reverse, opposite, contrary, anti- 反 反 反 反

合 口 kǒu	hé to combine, to join, to unite, to gather 合 合 合 合 合 合
合	
放 攵 pū	fàng to release, to liberate, to free 放 放 放 放 放 放 放 放
放	
做 亻 rén	zuò to work, to make, to act 做 做 做 做 做 做 做 做 做 做
做	
系 糸 mì	xì system, line, link, connection 系 系 系 系 系 系 系
系	
计 讠 yán	jì to calculate, to count, to plan, to reckon, plot, scheme 计 计 计 计
计	

或 戈 gē	**huò** or, either, else, maybe, perhaps, possibly 或 或 或 或 或 或 或 或
或	
司 口 kǒu	**sī** to take charge of, to control, to manage, officer 司 司 司 司 司
司	
利 刂 dāo	**lì** gains, advantage, profit, merit 利 利 利 利 利 利 利
利	
受 又 yòu	**shòu** to receive, to get, to accept, to bear 受 受 受 受 受 受 受 受
受	
光 儿 ér	**guāng** light, bright, brilliant, only, merely 光 光 光 光 光 光
光	

| 王 | wáng   king, ruler, royal, surname |
| 王
wáng | 王 王 王 王 |

| 王 | |

| 果 | guǒ   fruit, nut, result |
| 木
mù | 果 果 果 果 果 果 果 果 |

| 果 | |

| 亲 | qīn   relatives, parents, intimate, the hazelnut tree |
| 立
lì | 亲 亲 亲 亲 亲 亲 亲 亲 亲 |

| 亲 | |

| 界 | jiè   boundary, limit, domain, society, the world |
| 田
tián | 界 界 界 界 界 界 界 界 界 |

| 界 | |

| 及 | jí   to extend, to reach, and, in time |
| 又
yòu | 及 及 及 |

| 及 | |

今 人 rén	**jīn** modern, current, today, now 今 今 今 今
今	

京 亠 tóu	**jīng** capital city 京 京 京 京 京 京 京 京
京	

务 夂 zhǐ	**wù** affairs, business, should, must 务 务 务 务 务
务	

制 刂 dāo	**zhì** system, to establish, to manufacture, to overpower 制 制 制 制 制 制 制 制
制	

解 角 jiǎo	**jiě** to explain, to loosen, to unfasten, to untie 解 解 解 解 解 解 解 解 解 解 解
解	

各 口 kǒu	**gè** individual, each, every, all 各 各 各 各 各 各
各	
任 亻 rén	**rèn** to trust, to rely on, to appoint, to bear, duty, office 任 任 任 任 任 任
任	
至 至 zhì	**zhì** reach, arrive, very, extremely 至 至 至 至 至 至
至	
清 氵 shuǐ	**qīng** clean, pure, clear, distinct, peaceful 清 清 清 清 清 清 清 清 清 清 清
清	
物 牛 niú	**wù** thing, substance, matter, creature 物 物 物 物 物 物 物 物
物	

台 口 kǒu	tái — platform, unit, term of address 台 台 台 台 台
台	
象 豕 shǐ	xiàng — elephant, ivory, figure, image 象 象 象 象 象 象 象 象 象 象 象
象	
记 讠 yán	jì — mark, sign, to note, to record 记 记 记 记 记
记	
边 辶 chuò	biān — border, edge, margin, side 边 边 边 边 边
边	
共 八 bā	gòng — all, total, together, to share 共 共 共 共 共 共
共	

风 风 fēng	fēng wind, air, customs, manners, news 风 风 风 风
风	
战 戈 gē	zhàn war, fighting, battle 战 战 战 战 战 战 战 战 战
战	
干 十 shí	gàn arid, dry, to oppose, to offend, to invade 干 干 干
干	
接 扌 shǒu	jiē to connect, to join, to receive, to meet, to answer the phone 接 接 接 接 接 接 接 接 接 接
接	
它 宀 gài	tā it, other 它 它 它 它 它
它	

许 讠 yán	**xǔ** to consent, to permit, to promise, to betroth
八 八 bā	**bā** eight, all around, all sides
特 牛 niú	**tè** special, unique, distinguished
觉 见 jiàn	**jué** conscious, to nap, to sleep, to wake up
望 月 yuè	**wàng** to expect, to hope, to look forward to

直 目 mù	zhí straight, vertical, candid, direct, frank 直 直 直 直 直 直 直 直
直	
服 月 yuè	fú clothes, to dress, to wear, to take medicine 服 服 服 服 服 服 服 服
服	
毛 毛 máo	máo hair, fur, feathers, coarse 毛 毛 毛 毛
毛	
林 木 mù	lín forest, grove, surname 林 林 林 林 林 林 林 林
林	
题 页 yè	tí forehead, headline, title, theme 题 题 题 题 题 题 题 题 题 题 题 题 题 题 题
题	

建 又 yǐn	jiàn　　to build, to erect, to establish, to found
建	
南 十 shí	nán　　south, southern, southward
南	
度 广 guǎng	dù　　degree, system, manner, to consider
度	
统 纟 sī	tǒng　　to govern, to command, to gather, to unite
统	
色 色 sè	sè　　color, tint, hue, shade, beauty, form, sex
色	

字	zì — character, letter, symbol, word
子 zǐ	字 字 字 字 字 字

请	qǐng — to ask, to request, to invite, please
讠 yán	请 请 请 请 请 请 请 请 请 请

交	jiāo — to connect, to deliver, to exchange, to intersect, to mix
亠 tóu	交 交 交 交 交 交

爱	ài — to love, to like, to be fond of, love, affection
爫 zhǎo	爱 爱 爱 爱 爱 爱 爱 爱 爱 爱

让	ràng — to allow, to permit, to yield
讠 yán	让 让 让 让 让

认 讠 yán	rèn to know, to recognize, to understand 认 认 认 认							
认								
算 竹 zhú	suàn to calculate, to count, to figure, to plan 算 算 算 算 算 算 算 算 算 算 算 算 算 算							
算								
论 讠 yán	lùn debate, discussion 论 论 论 论 论 论							
论								
百 白 bái	bǎi one hundred, numerous, many 百 百 百 百 百 百							
百								
吃 口 kǒu	chī to eat, to drink, to suffer, to endure, to bear 吃 吃 吃 吃 吃 吃							
吃								

义 丿 piě	yì right conduct, propriety, justice
	义 义 义
义	
科 禾 hé	kē section, department, field, branch, science
	科 科 科 科 科 科 科 科 科
科	
怎 心 xīn	zěn what? why? how?
	怎 怎 怎 怎 怎 怎 怎 怎 怎
怎	
元 儿 ér	yuán first, dollar, origin, head
	元 元 元 元
元	
社 礻 shì	shè group, organization, society, a god of the soil
	社 社 社 社 社 社 社
社	

术 木 mù	shù skill, art, method, technique, trick 术 术 术 术 术
结 纟 sī	jié knot, tie, to connect, to join 结 结 结 结 结 结 结 结 结
六 八 bā	liù six 六 六 六 六
功 力 lì	gōng achievement, good work, merit, service 功 功 功 功 功
指 扌 shǒu	zhǐ finger, toe, to point, to indicate 指 指 指 指 指 指 指 指 指

思 心 xīn	sī to think, to ponder, to consider, final particle 思 思 思 思 思 思 思 思 思							
思								
非 非 fēi	fēi not, negative, non-, to oppose 非 非 非 非 非 非 非 非							
非								
流 氵 shuǐ	liú to flow, to drift, to circulate, class 流 流 流 流 流 流 流 流 流 流							
流								
每 母 mǔ	měi each, every 每 每 每 每 每 每 每							
每								
青 青 qīng	qīng nature's color, blue, green, black, young 青 青 青 青 青 青 青 青							
青								

管 ⺮ zhú	guǎn tube, pipe, duct, to manage, to control 管 管 管 管 管 管 管 管 管 管 管 管 管 管
管	
夫 大 dà	fū man, husband, worker, those 夫 夫 夫 夫
夫	
连 辶 chuò	lián to join, to connect, continuous, even 连 连 连 连 连 连 连
连	
远 辶 chuò	yuǎn distant, remote, far, profound 远 远 远 远 远 远 远
远	
资 贝 bèi	zī wealth, property, capital 资 资 资 资 资 资 资 资 资 资
资	

认 讠 yán	rèn to know, to recognize, to understand 认 认 认 认
认	
算 竹 zhú	suàn to calculate, to count, to figure, to plan 算 算 算 算 算 算 算 算 算 算 算 算 算 算
算	
论 讠 yán	lùn debate, discussion 论 论 论 论 论 论
论	
百 白 bái	bǎi one hundred, numerous, many 百 百 百 百 百 百
百	
吃 口 kǒu	chī to eat, to drink, to suffer, to endure, to bear 吃 吃 吃 吃 吃 吃
吃	

义 丿 piě	yì right conduct, propriety, justice 义 义 义							
义								
科 禾 hé	kē section, department, field, branch, science 科 科 科 科 科 科 科 科 科							
科								
怎 心 xīn	zěn what? why? how? 怎 怎 怎 怎 怎 怎 怎 怎 怎							
怎								
元 儿 ér	yuán first, dollar, origin, head 元 元 元 元							
元								
社 礻 shì	shè group, organization, society, a god of the soil 社 社 社 社 社 社 社							
社								

术 木 mù	shù skill, art, method, technique, trick 术 术 术 术 术
术	
结 纟 sī	jié knot, tie, to connect, to join 结 结 结 结 结 结 结 结 结
结	
六 八 bā	liù six 六 六 六 六
六	
功 力 lì	gōng achievement, good work, merit, service 功 功 功 功 功
功	
指 扌 shǒu	zhǐ finger, toe, to point, to indicate 指 指 指 指 指 指 指 指 指
指	

思 心 xīn	sī to think, to ponder, to consider, final particle 思 思 思 思 思 思 思 思 思
思	

非 非 fēi	fēi not, negative, non-, to oppose 非 非 非 非 非 非 非 非
非	

流 氵 shuǐ	liú to flow, to drift, to circulate, class 流 流 流 流 流 流 流 流 流 流
流	

每 母 mǔ	měi each, every 每 每 每 每 每 每 每
每	

青 青 qīng	qīng nature's color, blue, green, black, young 青 青 青 青 青 青 青 青
青	

管 竹 zhú	guǎn tube, pipe, duct, to manage, to control
	管 管 管 管 管 管 管 管 管 管 管 管 管 管

| 管 | | | | | | | | | |

夫 大 dà	fū man, husband, worker, those
	夫 夫 夫 夫

| 夫 | | | | | | | | | |

连 辶 chuò	lián to join, to connect, continuous, even
	连 连 连 连 连 连 连

| 连 | | | | | | | | | |

远 辶 chuò	yuǎn distant, remote, far, profound
	远 远 远 远 远 远 远

| 远 | | | | | | | | | |

资 贝 bèi	zī wealth, property, capital
	资 资 资 资 资 资 资 资 资 资

| 资 | | | | | | | | | |

运	yùn — to run, ship, transport, fortune, luck
辶 chuò	运 运 运 运 运 运 运
运	
武	wǔ — military, martial, warlike
止 zhǐ	武 武 武 武 武 武 武 武
武	
半	bàn — half, semi-, incomplete
十 shí	半 半 半 半 半
半	
候	hòu — to wait, to expect, to visit, to greet
亻 rén	候 候 候 候 候 候 候 候 候 候
候	
七	qī — seven
一 yī	七 七
七	

| 必
心
xīn | bì   surely, certainly, must, will |
| 必 | 必 必 必 必 必 |

| 城
土
tǔ | chéng   castle, city, town, municipality |
| 城 | 城 城 城 城 城 城 城 城 城 |

| 父
父
fù | fù   father, dad |
| 父 | 父 父 父 父 |

| 强
弓
gōng | qiáng   strong, powerful, energetic |
| 强 | 强 强 强 强 强 强 强 强 强 强 强 强 |

| 步
止
zhǐ | bù   walk, stroll, pace, march, to make progress |
| 步 | 步 步 步 步 步 步 步 |

完 宀 gài 完	wán to complete, to finish, to settle, whole
	完 完 完 完 完 完 完

革 革 gé 革	gé leather, animal hide, to reform, to remove
	革 革 革 革 革 革 革 革 革

深 氵 shuǐ 深	shēn deep, profound, depth
	深 深 深 深 深 深 深 深 深 深 深

区 匸 xì 区	qū area, district, region, ward, surname
	区 区 区 区

即 卩 jié 即	jí promptly, quickly, immediately
	即 即 即 即 即 即 即

求 水 shuǐ	qiú to seek, to request, to demand, to beseech, to beg for 求 求 求 求 求 求 求
求	
品 口 kǒu	pǐn article, good, product, commodity, quality, character 品 品 品 品 品 品 品 品 品
品	
士 士 shì	shì scholar, gentleman, soldier 士 士 士
士	
转 车 chē	zhuǎn to move, to convey, to turn, to revolve, to circle 转 转 转 转 转 转 转 转
转	
量 里 lǐ	liàng measure, volume, amount, quantity 量 量 量 量 量 量 量 量 量 量 量
量	

空 穴 xué	kōng hollow, empty, deserted, bare 空 空 空 空 空 空 空 空							
空								
甚 甘 gān	shén considerably, very, extremely, a great extent 甚 甚 甚 甚 甚 甚 甚 甚 甚							
甚								
众 人 rén	zhòng multitude, crowd, masses, public 众 众 众 众 众 众							
众								
技 扌 shǒu	jì ability, talent, skill, technique 技 技 技 技 技 技 技							
技								
轻 车 chē	qīng light, gentle, simple, easy 轻 轻 轻 轻 轻 轻 轻 轻 轻							
轻								

| 程 | chéng   process, rules, journey, trip, agenda, schedule |
| 禾 hé | 程 程 程 程 程 程 程 程 程 程 程 程 |

| 程 | | | | | | | | |

| 告 | gào   to tell, to inform, to announce, to accuse |
| 口 kǒu | 告 告 告 告 告 告 告 |

| 告 | | | | | | | | |

| 江 | jiāng   large river, the Yangtze, surname |
| 氵 shuǐ | 江 江 江 江 江 江 |

| 江 | | | | | | | | |

| 语 | yǔ   words, language, saying, expression |
| 讠 yán | 语 语 语 语 语 语 语 语 语 |

| 语 | | | | | | | | |

| 英 | yīng   petal, flower, leaf, brave, heroic, English |
| 艹 cǎo | 英 英 英 英 英 英 英 英 |

| 英 | | | | | | | | |

基 土 tǔ	jī foundation, base 基 基 基 基 基 基 基 基 基 基 基
派 氵 shuǐ	pài clique, faction, group, sect 派 派 派 派 派 派 派 派 派
满 氵 shuǐ	mǎn to fill, full, packed, satisfied 满 满 满 满 满 满 满 满 满 满 满 满
式 弋 yì	shì formula, pattern, rule, style, system 式 式 式 式 式 式
李 木 mù	lǐ plum, luggage, surname 李 李 李 李 李 李 李

| 息 | xī — to end, to cease, to put a stop to, pause, breath, rest, news |
| 心 xīn | 息 息 息 息 息 息 息 息 息 息 |

| 息 | |

| 写 | xiě — to write, to draw, to sketch, to compose |
| 冖 mì | 写 写 写 写 写 |

| 写 | |

| 呢 | né — wool, interrogative or emphatic final particle |
| 口 kǒu | 呢 呢 呢 呢 呢 呢 呢 呢 |

| 呢 | |

| 识 | shí — knowledge, to understand, to recognize, to know |
| 讠 yán | 识 识 识 识 识 识 识 |

| 识 | |

| 极 | jí — extreme, top, final, furthest, utmost, pole |
| 木 mù | 极 极 极 极 极 极 极 |

| 极 | |

令 人 rén	**lìng**　command, decree, order, magistrate, to allow, to cause 令 令 令 令 令
令	
黄 黄 huáng	**huáng**　yellow, surname 黄 黄 黄 黄 黄 黄 黄 黄 黄 黄 黄
黄	
德 彳 chì	**dé**　ethics, morality, compassion, kindness 德 德 德 德 德 德 德 德 德 德 德 德 德 德
德	
收 攵 pū	**shōu**　to collect, to gather, to harvest 收 收 收 收 收 收
收	
脸	**liǎn**　face, cheek, reputation 脸 脸 脸 脸 脸 脸 脸 脸 脸 脸 脸
脸	

钱 金 jīn	**qián** money, currency, coins 钱 钱 钱 钱 钱 钱 钱 钱 钱 钱
钱	
党 儿 ér	**dǎng** political party, gang, faction 党 党 党 党 党 党 党 党 党 党
党	
倒 亻 rén	**dào** to collapse, to fall over, to lie down 倒 倒 倒 倒 倒 倒 倒 倒 倒 倒
倒	
未 木 mù	**wèi** not yet, 8th terrestrial branch 未 未 未 未 未
未	
持 扌 shǒu	**chí** to hold, to support, to sustain 持 持 持 持 持 持 持 持 持
持	

取 又 yòu	qǔ to take, to receive, to obtain, to select 取取取取取取取取
设 讠 yán	shè to build, to design, to establish, to offer 设设设设设设
始 女 nǚ	shǐ to begin, to start, beginning 始始始始始始始始
版 片 piàn	bǎn printing block, edition, register, volume, version 版版版版版版版版
双 又 yòu	shuāng pair, couple, both, measure word for things that come in pairs 双双双双

历 厂 chǎng	lì history, calendar 历 历 历 历
历	
越 走 zǒu	yuè to exceed, to surpass, to transcend 越 越 越 越 越 越 越 越 越 越 越 越
越	
史 口 kǒu	shǐ history, chronicle, annals 史 史 史 史 史
史	
商 口 kǒu	shāng commerce, business, trade 商 商 商 商 商 商 商 商 商 商
商	
千 十 shí	qiān thousand, many, numerous, very 千 千 千
千	

片 片 piàn	piàn slice, splinter, page, strip 片 片 片 片
片	
容 宀 gài	róng appearance, looks, form, figure, to contain, to hold 容容容容容容容容容容
容	
研 石 shí	yán to grind, to rub, to study, to research 研研研研研研研研研
研	
像 亻 rén	xiàng picture, image, figure, to resemble 像像像像像像像像像像
像	
找 扌 shǒu	zhǎo to search for, to look for, to find, change (as in money) 找找找找找找找
找	

友 又 yòu	yǒu friend, companion, fraternity 友 友 友 友						
友							
孩 子 zi	hái baby, child, children 孩 孩 孩 孩 孩 孩 孩 孩 孩						
孩							
站 立 lì	zhàn stand, station, to halt, to stand, website 站 站 站 站 站 站 站 站 站 站						
站							
广 广 guǎng	guǎng broad, vast, wide, building, house 广 广 广						
广							
改 攵 pū	gǎi to alter, to change, to improve, to remodel 改 改 改 改 改 改 改						
改							

议 讠 yán	yì　　to consult, to talk over, to criticize, to discuss 议 议 议 议 议
议	

形 彡 shān	xíng　　form, shape, to appear, to describe, to look 形 形 形 形 形 形 形
形	

委 女 nǚ	wěi　　to appoint, to commission, to send 委 委 委 委 委 委 委 委
委	

早 日 rì	zǎo　　early, soon, morning 早 早 早 早 早 早
早	

房 户 hù	fáng　　building, house, room 房 房 房 房 房 房 房 房
房	

音 音 yīn	yīn sound, tone, pitch, pronunciation 音 音 音 音 音 音 音 音 音
音	
火 火 huǒ	huǒ fire, flame, to burn, anger, rage 火 火 火 火
火	
际 阝 yì	jì border, boundary, juncture 际 际 际 际 际 际 际
际	
则 刂 dāo	zé rule, law, regulation, grades 则 则 则 则 则 则
则	
首 首 shǒu	shǒu chief, head, leader 首 首 首 首 首 首 首 首 首
首	

单	dān — single, individual, only, lone
据	jù — to possess, to occupy, position, base
导	dǎo — to direct, to guide, to lead, to conduct
影	yǐng — shadow, image, reflection, photograph
失	shī — to lose, to make a mistake, to neglect

拿 手 shǒu	ná to bring, to grasp, to hold, to take 拿 拿 拿 拿 拿 拿 拿 拿 拿 拿
拿	
网 网 wǎng	wǎng net, network 网 网 网 网 网 网
网	
香 香 xiāng	xiāng incense, fragrant, aromatic 香 香 香 香 香 香 香 香 香
香	
似 亻 rén	shì resembling, similar to, as if, to seem 似 似 似 似 似 似
似	
斯 斤 jīn	sī this, thus, such, emphatic particle, used in transliterations 斯 斯 斯 斯 斯 斯 斯 斯 斯 斯 斯 斯
斯	

专 一 yī	zhuān concentrated, specialized, to monopolize 专 专 专 专
石 石 shí	shí stone, rock, mineral 石 石 石 石 石
若 艹 cǎo	ruò if, supposing, assuming, similar 若 若 若 若 若 若 若 若
兵 八 bā	bīng soldier, troops, an army, warlike 兵 兵 兵 兵 兵 兵 兵
弟 弓 gōng	dì young brother, junior 弟 弟 弟 弟 弟 弟 弟

谁 讠 yán	shuí — who? whom? whose? anyone? 谁 谁 谁 谁 谁 谁 谁 谁 谁 谁
谁	
校 木 mù	xiào — school, military field officer 校 校 校 校 校 校 校 校 校 校
校	
读 讠 yán	dú — to study, to learn, to read, to pronounce 读 读 读 读 读 读 读 读 读 读
读	
志 心 xīn	zhì — determination, will, mark, sign, to record, to write 志 志 志 志 志 志 志
志	
飞 飞 fēi	fēi — to fly, to dart, high 飞 飞 飞
飞	

| 观 | guān   to observe, to spectate, appearance, view |
| 见 jiàn | 观 观 观 观 观 观 |

| 观 | |

| 争 | zhēng   to dispute, to fight, to contend, to strive |
| 亅 jué | 争 争 争 争 争 争 |

| 争 | |

| 究 | jiū   to dig into, to investigate, actually, after all |
| 穴 xué | 究 究 究 究 究 究 究 |

| 究 | |

| 包 | bāo   wrap, pack, bundle, package |
| 勹 bāo | 包 包 包 包 包 |

| 包 | |

| 组 | zǔ   to form, to assemble, section, department |
| 纟 sī | 组 组 组 组 组 组 组 组 |

| 组 | |

造 辶 chuò	zào　　to build, to construct, to invent, to manufacture 造 造 造 造 造 造 造 造 造
造	
落 艹 cǎo	luò　　to fall, to drop, surplus, net income 落 落 落 落 落 落 落 落 落 落 落 落
落	
视 见 jiàn	shì　　to look at, to inspect, to observe, to regard 视 视 视 视 视 视 视 视
视	
济 氵 shuǐ	jì　　to aid, to help, to relieve, to ferry across 济 济 济 济 济 济 济 济
济	
喜 口 kǒu	xǐ　　to love, to enjoy, to be happy, joyful, glad 喜 喜 喜 喜 喜 喜 喜 喜 喜 喜 喜 喜
喜	

离 内 róu	lí　　rare beast, strange, elegant
	离 离 离 离 离 离 离 **离** 离 离
离	
虽 虫 chóng	suī　　although, even though
	虽 虽 虽 虽 虽 虽 虽 **虽** 虽
虽	
坐 土 tǔ	zuò　　seat, to sit, to ride, to travel by
	坐 坐 坐 坐 坐 坐 **坐**
坐	
集 隹 zhuī	jí　　to gather, to collect, set, collection
	集 集 集 集 集 集 集 集 **集** 集 集 集
集	
编 纟 sī	biān　　to knit, to weave, to arrange, to compile
	编 编 编 编 编 编 编 编 **编** 编 编 编
编	

宝 宀 gài 宝	**bǎo**　treasure, jewel, rare, precious 宝宝宝宝宝宝宝宝
谈 讠 yán 谈	**tán**　to talk, to chat, conversation, surname 谈谈谈谈谈谈谈谈谈谈
府 广 guǎng 府	**fǔ**　prefect, prefecture, government 府府府府府府府府
拉 扌 shǒu 拉	**lā**　to pull, to drag, to seize, to hold, to lengthen, to play (a violin) 拉拉拉拉拉拉拉拉
黑 黑 hēi 黑	**hēi**　black, dark, evil, sinister 黑黑黑黑黑黑黑黑黑黑黑黑

且 一 yī	**qiě** moreover, also (post-subject), about to, will soon (pre-verb) 且 且 且 且 且
且	
随 阝 yì	**suí** to follow, to listen to, to submit to 随 随 随 随 随 随 随 随 随 随 随
随	
格 木 mù	**gé** form, pattern, standard 格 格 格 格 格 格 格 格 格 格
格	
尽 尸 shī	**jǐn** to exhaust, to use up, to deplete 尽 尽 尽 尽 尽 尽
尽	
剑 刂 dāo	**jiàn** sword, dagger, saber 剑 剑 剑 剑 剑 剑 剑 剑 剑
剑	

讲 讠 yán 讲	jiǎng talk, speech, lecture, to speak, to explain 讲 讲 讲 讲 讲 讲
布 巾 jīn 布	bù cotton, linen, textiles, to announce, to declare, to spread 布 布 布 布 布
杀 木 mù 杀	shā to kill, to murder, to slaughter, to hurt 杀 杀 杀 杀 杀 杀
微 彳 chì 微	wēi small, tiny, trifling, micro- 微 微 微 微 微 微 微 微 微 微 微 微
怕 忄 xīn 怕	pà to fear, to be afraid of, apprehensive 怕 怕 怕 怕 怕 怕 怕 怕

母	mǔ — mother, female elders, female
母 mǔ	母 母 母 母 母
母	
调	diào — tune, melody, key, to transfer, to exchange
讠 yán	调 调 调 调 调 调 调 调 调 调
调	
局	jú — bureau, office, circumstance, game, situation
尸 shī	局 局 局 局 局 局 局
局	
根	gēn — root, basis, foundation
木 mù	根 根 根 根 根 根 根 根 根 根
根	
曾	céng — already, formerly, once, the past
曰 yuē	曾 曾 曾 曾 曾 曾 曾 曾 曾 曾 曾 曾
曾	

准 冫 **bīng** 准	zhǔn standard, accurate, to permit, to approve, to allow 准 准 准 准 准 准 准 准 准 准
团 囗 **wéi** 团	tuán sphere, circle, ball, mass, lump, group, regiment, to gather 团 团 团 团 团 团
段 殳 **shū** 段	duàn section, piece, division 段 段 段 段 段 段 段 段 段
终 纟 **sī** 终	zhōng end, finally, in the end 终 终 终 终 终 终 终 终
乐 丿 **piě** 乐	lè cheerful, happy, laughing, music 乐 乐 乐 乐 乐

切 刀 dāo	qiè　　to cut, to mince, to slice, to carve, close to, eager 切 切 切 切
切	
级 纟 sī	jí　　level, rank, class, grade 级 级 级 级 级 级
级	
克 儿 ér	kè　　to subdue, to restrain, to overcome, used in transliterations 克 克 克 克 克 克 克
克	
精 米 mǐ	jīng　　essence, germ, spirit 精 精 精 精 精 精 精 精 精 精 精 精
精	
哪 口 kǒu	nǎ　　which? where? how? 哪 哪 哪 哪 哪 哪 哪 哪 哪
哪	

官 宀 gài	guān official, public servant 官 官 官 官 官 官 官 官
官	
示 示 shì	shì altar, ceremony, to show, to demonstrate 示 示 示 示 示
示	
冲 冫 bīng	chōng wash, rinse, flush, dash, soar 冲 冲 冲 冲 冲 冲
冲	
竟 立 lì	jìng finally, after all, at last, indeed, unexpected 竟 竟 竟 竟 竟 竟 竟 竟 竟 竟
竟	
乎 丿 piě	hū interrogative or exclamatory final particle 乎 乎 乎 乎 乎
乎	

www.ingramcontent.com/pod-product-compliance
Lightning Source LLC
Chambersburg PA
CBHW080718120726
48001CB00010B/3065